Contents

D0258477

Introduction

Writing without pencils

Writing without pencils is one of a series of books containing 'outside the box' ideas for practitioners working with children in the early years. Children's interests and joy for life form the basis for the activities in this series. The activities build on children's natural instinct to be doing, investigating, making, creating and solving problems. They are designed to excite and stimulate children as they learn through their senses, being active and thinking for themselves.

But why writing without pencils?

What is wrong with a pencil on a sheet of paper? The answer is, of course, nothing at all. But it is good practice to reflect on the benefits of writing activities and ask: *Is this the best way to encourage very young children to want to write? Could there be other ways to inspire them?*

Children love variety so introducing something unexpected can be the catalyst needed to spark an idea and capture their imaginations. The activities in this book are designed to give practitioners ideas to provide varied opportunities for writing as part of creative, imaginative and role play situations – indoors and outside. They are not purely writing activities, but an integral part of cross-curricular fun that focus on opportunities for writing in unusual forms.

Wanting to write

In these activities, children are encouraged to develop their use of language through participating in a range of experiences which give them a reason to want to write. Actually 'wanting to write' is the key to a child's success. If young children are motivated to want to write, then they will find a way to communicate, express their ideas and find enjoyment in the experience of writing.

How to use this book

The book is organised into three sections:
● Chapter 1: 'Forming letters' includes ideas to enable children to experiment with

Writing without pencils

Writing with torches, icing, fingers and more

For ages
3-5

Brenda Whittle

Author
Brenda Whittle

Editor
Kate Element

Assistant Editor
Rachel Mackinnon

Series Designer
Anna Oliwa

Designer
Yen Fu and
Anna Oliwa

Cover Illustration
Craig Cameron/
The Art Collection

Illustrations
Debbie Clark

Text © 2007 Brenda Whittle
© 2007 Scholastic Ltd

Designed using Adobe InDesign

Published by Scholastic Ltd
Villiers House
Clarendon Avenue
Leamington Spa
Warwickshire
CV32 5PR

www.scholastic.co.uk

Printed by Bell & Bain

1 2 3 4 5 6 7 8 9   7 8 9 0 1 2 3 4 5 6

British Library Cataloguing-in-Publication Data
A catalogue record for this book is available from the British Library.

ISBN 0-439-94499-6
ISBN 978-0439-94499-1

Acknowledgements
The publishers gratefully acknowledge permission to reproduce the following copyright material:
Julie Boden for the use of 'Welly Walking' by Julie Boden © 2007, Julie Boden (previously unpublished).
Qualifications and Curriculum Authority for the uses of extracts from the QCA/DfEE document *Curriculum guidance for the foundation stage* © 2000 Qualifications and Curriculum Authority.
Every effort has been made to trace copyright holders for the works reproduced in this book, and the publishers apologise for any inadvertent omissions.

Due to the nature of the web, we cannot guarantee the content or links of any site mentioned. We strongly recommend that teachers check websites before using them in the classroom.

pre-writing activities, mark-making, letter formation and linking sounds to letters. These activities include going camping and writing with torchlight, icing letters onto biscuits and writing letters in the play area big enough to ride along on wheeled toys. Some of the extension ideas include writing their names and some words.

● Chapter 2: 'Reasons for writing' includes a wide variety of activities such as writing messages in sand, simple instructions for an outdoor game, signs, captions, lists, labels and making simple books. The extension ideas include writing sentences.

● Chapter 3: 'Writing stories and poems' includes different starting points to capture children's imaginations in creative writing. They include making up a story from clues, putting pieces of a puzzle together to sequence a story and writing poems on a bunch of bananas and a line of washing.

The activities
Planning and learning objectives

Links to the Stepping Stones and Early Learning Goals for Communication, language and literacy in the QCA document *Curriculum guidance for the foundation stage* are shown for each activity to aid planning. The activities are all cross-curricular and the main link to one of the other five Areas of Learning is also shown where appropriate.

Support and extension

Each activity has suggestions for how it may be adapted or extended, according to children's needs and stage of development.

Assessment

Practitioners can assess children's progress against the Stepping Stones and Early Learning Goals shown for each activity. Most of the activities are designed for small groups, enabling practitioners to observe individual children's progress and aid assessment to inform future planning.

Further activities

These provide more suggestions for developing lively ideas linked to the main activity.

Play links

Ideas for play-linked learning to the main activity are given to continue the theme into other Areas of Learning, such as opportunities for investigations or role play.

Home links

In order to promote and foster a partnership with parents or carers for the benefit of the children, a suggestion is given in each activity to link the learning in the setting with that in the home.

Health and safety

When working outside, always check that the area is clean and safe, and that children wash their hands after collecting items such as leaves. Ensure to check with parents and carers that children do not have any allergies before tasting foods, touching plants or using glues and soap.

Abbreviations

References to Areas of Learning in the QCA document *Curriculum guidance for the foundation stage*:
● Personal, social and emotional development **(PSED)**
● Communication, language and literacy **(CLL)**
● Mathematical development **(MD)**
● Knowledge and understanding of the world **(KUW)**
● Physical development **(PD)**
● Creative development **(CD)**

Forming letters

Torchlight

In this activity the children go on an adventure, pretending that it is night-time. They use the beams of light from their torches as writing equipment and practise drawing lines with large arm movements. The adventure provides a perfect opportunity to develop language and writing through imaginative play.

Early writers make writing patterns and write the initial letters in their names.
More confident writers identify and write the letters they see in the signs along the journey and list the animals they have seen.

What you need

Selection of small torches; darkened area such as a tent or a den made from blankets or fabric draped over tables or clothes airers; signs saying 'The dark forest', 'The campsite', 'Stony River' and 'Blue Top Mountains', arranged along the route you want to take, with 'The campsite' as the last sign.

What to do

● Explain to the children that you are going to imagine that you will be setting out on an adventure at night-time. Ask the children what they could take with them to help them see where they are going. Let each child choose a torch. Talk about the journey and tell the children that you will be going through the 'dark forest', along the side of 'Stony River', over the 'Blue Top Mountains' to the 'campsite'.

● When you reach the tent, go inside and ask the children to use the beam of light from their torches to write the first letter of their names on the side of the tent, as a signal telling anyone else in the campsite that they have arrived. Then give the children time to experiment with using the beams of light from their torches to write letters or make patterns.

● Before leaving the tent,

Learning objectives
Stepping Stones
● Draw lines and circles using gross motor movement. **(CLL)**
● Begin to form recognisable letters. **(CLL)**
Early Learning Goal
● Form recognisable letters, most of which are correctly formed. **(CLL)**

ask each child to write the first letter of their name and draw a big circle on the wall of the tent to signal that they are now leaving the campsite.

Support and extension
● Younger children can trace over large pre-drawn letters with the beam of light from their torches.
● Ask older children to see if they recognise any of the letters in the signs used on the journey. Ask them to tell you the sounds of the letters and to write them on the wall with the light from their torches.

Further activities
● Write the names of some animals you might have seen on the journey, such as pig, cat, dog, fox, hen or sheep. Ask the children to help you by taking it in turns to write the first sound in the animal names using their torchlight on black paper. Then write the whole word using yellow chalk. More confident writers can write the words themselves.
● Talk about the different types of light in the sky at night. Tell the children that they are going to write their names, or the first letter

of their names in stars. Buy or make your own stars from silver or yellow paper, and encourage the children to write with these on dark blue paper.

Play link
Set up a role-play area inside or outside, where the children can imagine they are camping. Provide a tent, a blanket, a cardboard box to use as a camping stove, cooking utensils and play food. Leave a box of recycled objects such as plastic containers, packaging materials and cardboard tubes, nearby for the children to use if they want to incorporate their own resources into their play. **(CLL)**

Home link
Suggest that parents or carers provide their children with small, inexpensive torches as a different and inspiring way of encouraging them to make patterns and write letters.

Cross-curricular links
Stepping Stones
● Know how to operate simple equipment. **(KUW)**
● Use one-handed tools and equipment. **(PD)**
Early Learning Goals
● Find out about and identify the uses of everyday technology. **(KUW)**
● Handle tools, objects safely with increasing control. **(PD)**

7

Yummy letters

In this role play situation the children imagine that it is their first day working as a cake decorator in a baker's shop. They learn to follow instructions and write letters on cakes or biscuits using an icing pen.

What you need

Selection of small iced cakes or biscuits; icing tubes or pens in different colours (these are readily available in the baking section of supermarkets); 'The cake shop' photocopiable page 9, enlarged to A3; aprons; hand-washing facilities.

What to do

● If possible, arrange a visit to a baker's shop to look at the iced cakes and biscuits that are for sale. Give the children time to talk about the sights and smells. Ask them to choose a selection of small, decorated cakes or biscuits to take back to the setting. If a visit is not possible, bring in a selection of cakes or biscuits and ask the children to look at the ways in which they are decorated. Can they say what they like and why? Check with parents and carers first for any food allergies or dietary requirements before allowing children to handle any food.

● Ask the children to imagine that today is their first day at work in a baker's shop as a cake decorator. Read the step-by-step instructions together on how to decorate biscuits from the photocopiable sheet.

● Talk about the importance of hygiene when handling food and ensure that they

Early writers make marks and writing patterns on top of a large cake.
More confident writers practise writing their names on greaseproof paper using the icing pen.

all wash their hands and wear clean aprons. Let the children choose an icing tube and experiment with writing letters on the biscuits. They can choose different coloured icing to add dots or patterns.

● When the icing is dry, pack the biscuits along with some drinks to share on a picnic together. Ask the children to tell you any of the letter sounds which they recognise before eating the biscuits. (Check again for allergies.)

Support and extension

● Invite younger children to ice patterns on top of a large cake as a pre-writing activity.
● Encourage older children to write their names on greaseproof paper using the icing tubes.

Further activities

● Ask the children to ice one biscuit for each letter of the word 'picnic'. Write the word 'picnic' on a large sheet of paper and let the children match the biscuits to the appropriate letters before eating them.
● Ice patterns on to star-shaped biscuits and let the children add silver confectionery balls for sparkle.

Home link

Suggest that parents and carers let their children look at the wide range of biscuits available in supermarkets and choose a small packet to share, if appropriate.

Learning objectives
Stepping Stones
● Begin to form recognisable letters. **(CLL)**
● Hear and say the initial sound in words and know which letters represent some of the sounds. **(CLL)**
Early Learning Goals
● Form recognisable letters, most of which are correctly formed. **(CLL)**
● Link sounds to letters, naming and sounding the letters of the alphabet. **(CLL)**

Cross-curricular links
Stepping Stone
● Use one-handed tools and equipment. **(PD)**
Early Learning Goal
● Handle tools, objects safely and with increasing control. **(PD)**

The Cake Shop

How to ice cakes and biscuits:

1. Wash your hands.

2. Put on a clean apron.

red   green   blue

3. Choose the colour of icing.

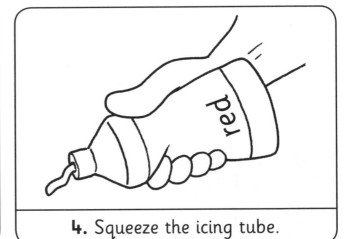

red

4. Squeeze the icing tube.

5. Draw a letter on the cake or biscuit.

6. Leave to dry.

SCHOLASTIC
www.scholastic.co.uk

Growing letters

**This activity provides opportunities to develop fine motor control
as the children write letters in compost with their fingers or sticks
and shake seeds from a packet on to the letters.**

Early writers are motivated to practise and improve their manipulative skills which later aid handwriting. **More confident writers** develop skills in writing by compiling lists using a word processing programme.

What you need

Large shallow seed trays; compost; cress seeds; small sticks; selection of leafy vegetables or herbs including lettuce, watercress, parsley and cress.

What to do

● Before you begin this activity check with parents and carers for any allergies to plants or compost. Ask the children if they can name some leafy vegetables or herbs which they can eat. Show them examples and see if they can name them. Talk about the importance of green vegetables in a healthy diet. Discuss which vegetables the children enjoy and how they eat them.

● Explain that all of these vegetables and herbs grow from seeds. Tell the children that they are going to grow cress from seeds and that given the right conditions, it will grow quickly and they can eat it.

● Let the children put handfuls of compost into the seed tray, making a layer approximately 3cm deep. Encourage them to describe what the compost feels like.

● Ask the children to write letters of their names or the names of the vegetables in the compost, using their fingers or a stick to form them. Reinforce that they should wash their hands immediately after touching the compost.

● Smooth over the compost and cut a small hole in one corner of a cress seed

Learning objectives
Stepping Stones
● Begin to form recognisable letters. **(CLL)**
● Manipulate objects with increasing control. **(CLL)**
● Ascribe meaning to marks. **(CLL)**
Early Learning Goals
● Form recognisable letters, most of which are correctly formed. **(CLL)**
● Write their own names and other things such as labels and captions. **(CLL)**

packet. Do not let the children use seeds which have been chemically treated. Ask the children to use their fingers to write the initial letter of their name in the compost and then shake the seeds on to the channels they have created.

● If you have enough seeds, the children could write the word 'cress' in the compost of another seed tray. Water the seeds and watch them grow into the letter shapes over the next few days. When the cress is fully grown you can cut it, rinse it and eat in a sandwich, ensuring to check for any food allergies beforehand.

Support and extension

● Invite younger children to draw large patterns and letter shapes in the compost with sticks and spend time exploring its qualities.

● Older children can list vegetables and herbs using a word processing program and add images to illustrate their work.

Further activities

● Try growing other seeds such as radishes, which can be sown in large pots in letter shapes.

● Make a 'letter garden' by placing a layer of compost in a shallow tray and pressing pebbles into the compost to form the letters. Add leaves, small flowers and twigs to make a garden.

Play link

Provide a tray of compost, an assortment of plastic flower pots, seed trays, spoons, trowels, watering can and inexpensive artificial flowers. As the children fill the pots and trays, ask questions such as: *Which pot holds the most compost? Which containers are best for the flowers? Why? What happens when you add a lot of water to a pot of compost? How many spoonfuls of compost do you need to fill a small plant pot?* and so on.
(KUW, MD)

Home link

Suggest that parents and carers encourage their children to look at the wide variety of vegetables available when they go shopping and try to name as many as possible.

Cross-curricular links
Stepping Stone
● Examine objects and living things to find out more about them. **(KUW)**
Early Learning Goal
● Investigate objects and materials by using all of their senses as appropriate. **(KUW)**

Sky writing

This is a good activity to try on a clear day when children are full of energy and you all want to go outside. Children will learn correct letter formation by using large arm movements to form letters in the air, and identify and run around letters drawn on the ground.

What you need

Safe, open space; lengths of rope (such as skipping ropes); 'Aeroplanes' photocopiable page 13; blanket; scissors.

What to do

● Ask the children what they would expect to see in the sky. Have they ever noticed 'lines in the sky' or vapour trails left by aeroplanes? On a warm, clear day, take a blanket and ask the children to lie down and look at the sky, making sure that they are looking away from the Sun. Remind them that they should never look directly at the Sun as it would be harmful to their eyes.

● Explain that by looking at vapour trails we can see the path which the aeroplane has taken. Ask the children to imagine that they are pilots and to run around making patterns as if they are flying aeroplanes in straight, curved or looped lines. Encourage them to use all the space available and avoid bumping into each other.

● Invite each child to cut out a card aeroplane from the photocopiable sheet. Show them how to hold the aeroplanes in their hands to draw lines, circles (using an anticlockwise movement) or form letters in the air using large arm movements. Remind the children to form the letters correctly.

● Take it in turns to write a letter of the alphabet in the air and ask the rest of the group to try and identify it. Use the ropes to make the 'sky writing' letters and patterns on the ground instead of in the sky, and encourage them to run around the ropes carefully, making sure not to bump in to each other.

> **Early writers** learn to make up and down letter movements and draw circles with an anticlockwise movement. **More confident writers** write letters on to paper using glue and string.

Learning objectives

Stepping Stone
● Draw lines and circles using gross motor movement. **(CLL)**
Early Learning Goal
● Form recognisable letters, most of which are correctly formed. **(CLL)**

Support and extension

● For younger children, draw large patterns or letters on the playground using chalk and let them run along these. Ask them to find a wavy pattern, run along a zigzag or stand in the middle of the letter 'o'.

● Ask older children to glue their aeroplane on to the left-hand side of a piece of blue paper and write a letter behind the aeroplane using a glue stick. Place string on the glue to represent the vapour trail the plane has left behind.

Further activity

● On black paper, paint words in silver that are linked to the theme such as 'plane', 'fast', 'sky' or 'clouds'. Do the children think they would be able to see vapour trails at night?

Home links

Let the children take a card aeroplane home to show their parents and carers how they form letters using them. Suggest that they look for vapour trails in the sky on the way to the setting.

Cross-curricular links

Stepping Stone
● Show respect for other children's personal space when playing among them. **(PD)**
Early Learning Goal
● Show awareness of space, of themselves and of others. **(PD)**

Aeroplanes

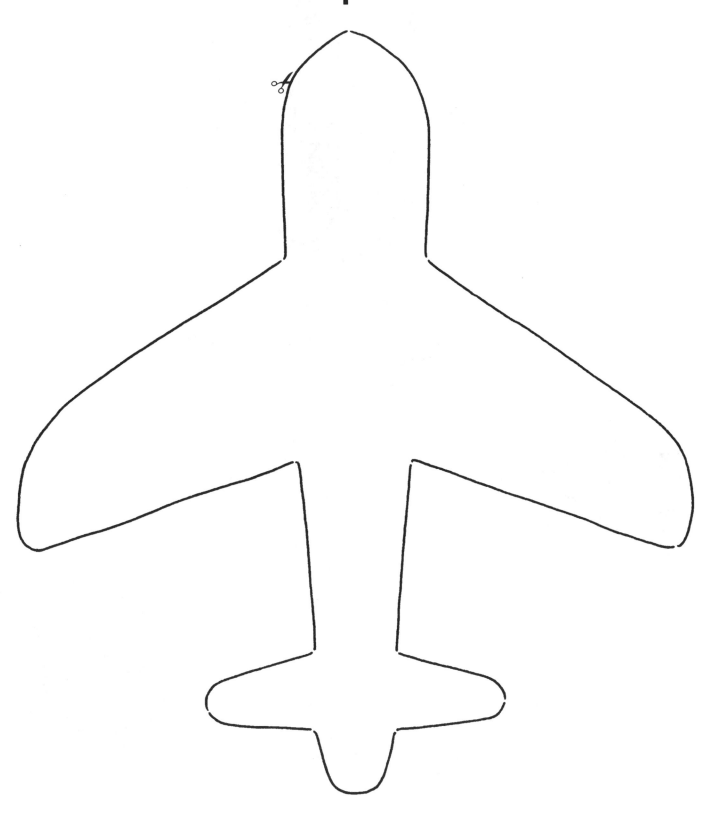

SCHOLASTIC
www.scholastic.co.uk

Stitch it

In this activity, children have the opportunity to touch, describe and sort fabrics and threads, before mark-making and writing their names using a needle and thread.

Early writers thread laces through lacing cards, developing fine motor skills.
More confident writers use chalk to write their names on fabric and sew over the letters using a running stitch.

What you need

A collection of open weave fabrics such as hessian; large-eyed blunt needles; assorted thick threads and wools; decorative items such as buttons, sequins and ribbons; scissors; adult helpers; glue.

What to do

● Show the children the collection of fabrics, threads and decorative items. Let them touch and explore the textures and colours. Ask the children to sort the collection in different ways, for example, by colour, type, texture or 'my favourites'. Encourage the use of descriptive language such as 'scratchy', 'smooth', or 'silky'.
● Show the children the sewing needles and ask them if they can think of a way to make marks or write letters by just using the

materials in front of them. Show the children how to thread a needle and make simple running stitches. Although the needles are blunt, remind the children how to use them safely.
● Invite each child to choose a piece of fabric and thread. Help thread the needles and let the children experiment in making marks with their stitches. Their stitching can be random or they may be able to complete a running stitch. For this activity to be successful and satisfying for the children, you will need extra adult assistance with the unravelling of threads and re-threading of needles. Perhaps parents or carers could be invited to help.
● Ask the children to glue

Learning objectives
Stepping Stones
● Engage in activities requiring hand-eye coordination. **(CLL)**
● Ascribe meaning to marks. **(CLL)**
Early Learning Goals
● Form recognisable letters, most of which are correctly formed. **(CLL)**
● Write their own names and other things such as labels and captions. **(CLL)**

buttons or sequins on to the fabric to form the first letter of their names. They can also add more items to decorate their work around the stitching.

Support and extension
● Younger children can thread laces through the holes in lacing cards purchased through educational suppliers.
● Encourage older children to write their names on fabric using chalk and sewing over the letters using running stitches.

Further activities
● Provide squares of hessian approximately 10cm square as a basis for collage work. Ask the children to choose and cut pieces of open weave fabric and attach these to the hessian using simple running stitches. Mount the finished squares together to make a patchwork picture.
● Provide thick string, plastic clothes lines and skipping ropes. Ask the children to 'sew' in and out through the spaces in a garden fence or lattice work.

Play link
Provide two metre lengths of fabrics of differing textures and colours which you think will appeal to the children. These could include shiny, silky, furry, rough or sheer fabrics. Display them attractively in a basket and leave the children to play with them as they wish. They may wrap the fabric around themselves and become imaginary characters, 'draw' with it by using it as a line to make shapes, cover themselves with it or just enjoy the tactile qualities. Vary play opportunities by adding different items such as clothes pegs, scarves and belts, crowns, a box of 'jewels' (shiny beads and buttons) and story books about kings and queens. **(CD)**

Home link
Ask the children to bring in any fabric scraps from home to use in sewing and collage work.

Cross-curricular links
Stepping Stone
● Begin to try out a range of tools and techniques safely. **(KUW)**
Early Learning Goal
● Select the tools and techniques they need to shape, assemble and join materials they are using. **(KUW)**

Letter track

Children have the chance to write on different scales, varying from tiny letters to enormous letters drawn in chalk on the playground, which they can then ride along on wheeled toys.

Early writers swirl ribbons in the air using large shoulder movements to write letters and make patterns.
More confident writers write giant letters on the playground to use as tracks for wheeled toys.

What you need
Outdoor play area; chalk; ride-on wheeled toys; markers such as cones.

What to do
● Before the session, draw the letter 's' using chalk in several places in the play area, making sure that each letter is big enough for the children to ride tricycles or other toys along the line. Put a marker such as a cone at the top of each letter to show the starting point.
● This activity can be adapted to fit in with the introduction of a new letter sound. It is particularly suitable for introducing the letters, 'c', 'e', 'l', 'o', 's', 'v', 'w' and 'z'.
● Introduce 's' as a letter sound and ask the

children to find and bring into the setting an object which has 's' as the initial sound in its name. Say the names of the objects together, giving the children the opportunity to enjoy saying the 's' sound at the beginning of each word.
● Form the letter 's' shape in the air together – emphasising the starting place. Draw it big with large shoulder movements and little using smaller movements with a finger. Next, ask the children to use their fingers to write a tiny 's' on the floor or table. Repeat these steps, this time with eyes closed.
● Make the activity fun and

Learning objectives
Stepping Stones
● Begin to form recognisable letters. **(CLL)**
● Hear and say the initial sound in words and know which letters represent some of the sounds. **(CLL)**
Early Learning Goals
● Form recognisable letters, most of which are correctly formed. **(CLL)**
● Link sounds to letters, naming and sounding the letters of the alphabet. **(CLL)**

part of a game, for example, *Make the biggest 's' you can. Make the smallest 's' you can. Write an 's' on your leg/your friend's back/under the table* and so on.

● Finally, ask the children to make the biggest letter 's' they can. Tell them that you have a way that they can make an even bigger letter. Show them the letters drawn in the play area. Remind them that they start writing the letter 's' from the top and that the cones are there to remind them to start from that point when they travel along the letters on the ride-on toys. Ask the children to ride slowly, trying to stay on the lines.

● Repeat the activity with other letters as appropriate.

Support and extension

● Ask younger children to hold one end of a ribbon in their hands and write letters or make wavy, snake patterns in the air. Draw long snakes in the play area for them to ride along.

● Older children can draw and ride along letters which they have drawn in the play area themselves.

Further activity

● Ask the children to paint letters or words on an A3 paper. They can then use these letters as race tracks and trace over the letter shapes using toy cars. To help with letter formation, make starting flags and ask the children to glue these where the car should start the race.

Play link

Give children the opportunity to examine objects and see how they work by setting up a simple garage area with a variety of different sized wheeled vehicles, tools and assorted plastic containers that can be used as containers for oil or water for the vehicles. Add notepads and pens for the children to write bills and messages. **(KUW)**

Home link

Suggest that parents help children to find objects at the home which begin with a particular letter sound.

Cross-curricular links
Stepping Stone
● Persevere in repeating some actions/attempts when developing a new skill. **(PD)**
Early Learning Goal
● Show awareness of space, of themselves and of others. **(PD)**

Wet and watery

This warm weather activity provides opportunities for children to practise early letter formation skills as they form large letters and words in the play area by pouring water from containers.

Early writers learn to use anticlockwise movements to form the letter 'o' and to work from left to right. **More confident writers** write words and messages.

What you need

Outdoor play area; water tray; plastic bowls; assorted plastic containers such as jugs, bottles, sieves, tubes, plant sprayers and funnels.

What to do

● Set up a water area outside with space for children to play on a hard surface. For safety reasons, any form of water play must be closely supervised at all times. Give the children time to play freely with the water and containers, pouring, sifting and squirting. When they have had time to experiment on their own, ask questions such as: *How can I pour water from this big tub into this small bottle? Will this sieve float? What shape is water?* and so on.

● Ask the children to fill the plastic containers with water and to experiment in making patterns and lines by pouring water on to the play surface. Let them touch the wet and dry areas and talk about the difference. Will the wet areas stay wet?

● Gather the children together and using a jug of water, slowly pour water on to the play surface to form a large letter 'w'. Ask if they recognise the letter and can identify its sound. Ask them for words beginning with 'w', include 'wet' and 'water' in the list. Give the children the opportunity to write this letter, pouring water slowly and carefully from small plastic jugs.

● Exchange the jugs for narrow-topped plastic bottles and show the

Learning objectives
Stepping Stones
● Draw lines and circles using gross motor movements. **(CLL)**
● Begin to use anticlockwise movement. **(CLL)**
● Hear and say the initial sounds in words and know which letters represent some of the sounds. **(CLL)**
Early Learning Goals
● Form recognisable letters, most of which are correctly formed. **(CLL)**
● Link sounds to letters, naming and sounding the letters of the alphabet. **(CLL)**

children how to draw a big circle or letter 'o', starting at the top and working in an anticlockwise direction. Ask them to write a long line of the letter 'o' working from left to right. This early practice will help when they learn the letters 'a', 'c', 'd', 'g', 'o' and 'q'.

Support and extension

● Draw circles and patterns using chalk for younger children to follow when they are writing.
● Older children can use small squeezy bottles filled with water to write words beginning with a given letter or to write messages. Will the message still be there later in the day?

Further activities

● Provide the children with small buckets of water and large paint brushes. Ask them to write their names in the outside play area on the ground or on a wall or fence.
● Give the children time to experiment in spraying water from plant sprayers on to the play area and painting lines with water. Remind children of this experience when, at a later time, they are using the spray tool and paintbrush in a simple paint package on the computer, illustrating how they are linked.

Play links

● Give children the opportunity to find out about capacity by giving them time to play with a water tray filled with buckets, bowls and bottles of different sizes. Challenge them to work things out for themselves. Will all the water from the bucket go into the bowl? If you fill all the bottles and empty them into the bucket, will it be full? Which container holds the most water? **(MD)**
● On a warm, windy day set up an area where the children can wash the dolls' clothes and peg them on to a line. Also let them pour buckets of water on to the play area and use long handled brushes to scrub it clean. Will the clothes and the play area stay wet all day? Examine them later. What has happened? How did they dry out? **(KUW)**

Home link

Suggest that parents or carers encourage water play at bath time by adding safe and clean plastic containers such as empty drinks and shampoo bottles, margarine tubs and plastic spoons.

Cross-curricular links
Stepping Stone
● Demonstrate increasing skill and control in the use of mark-making implements. **(PD)**
Early Learning Goal
● Handle tools, objects, construction and malleable materials safely and with increasing control. **(PD)**

Run around

Children learn on the move in this activity, as they search for objects beginning with 'b' and learn to form the letter correctly by running around a giant letter 'b' in the play area.

What you need

'Buzzy bees' photocopiable page 21; skipping ropes; cones; objects beginning with the letter 'b' placed around the room; glue or similar to stick 'bees' to objects.

Early writers 'buzz' around finding objects beginning with the sound 'b' and linking these to the letter 'b'.
More confident writers make other letters from ropes in the play area.

What to do

● Choose a particular letter to be the focus of this activity. When writing the letter' b',

Learning objectives
Stepping Stones
● Draw lines and circles using gross motor movement. **(CLL)**
● Hear and say the initial sound in words and know which letters represent some of the sounds. **(CLL)**
Early Learning Goals
● Form recognisable letters, most of which are correctly formed. **(CLL)**
● Hear and say initial and final sounds in words, and short vowel sounds within words. **(CLL)**

children often find difficulty in forming the letter correctly and write it as a number six. Try using this activity to reinforce the correct letter formation.
● Show the children the photocopiable sheet and ask them to tell you the initial sound of the word 'bee'. Give each child one of the bees and ask them to buzz around the room with you looking for objects beginning with 'b'. Let the children stick a bee to each object.
● Show the children how to write a letter 'b' in the air, moving their arms from the shoulder. Ask them to cover the room in the letter 'b' by drawing on objects using their fingers. Check they are forming the letters correctly.
● Go outside and together make a giant letter 'b' using skipping ropes. Ask the

children to take it in turns to walk alongside the rope showing the correct way to write the letter. Invite them to use the cones and ropes to make more examples of the letter 'b' themselves.
● When the letters are completed, ask the children to 'write' the letter 'b' by running around the letters, remembering to form them correctly.

Support and extension

● Hold hands with a younger child and run around the letters together.
● Older children can make other letters using ropes and cones and run around them to show you that they can form them correctly.

Further activity

● Give each child one of the bees and ask them to hold it high in the air and say 'Buzz!' whenever they hear you saying a word beginning with 'b'. Either call out words or read part of a favourite story that has lots of 'b' words.

Home link

Give the photocopiable sheet to parents and carers to help their children find six items in the home beginning with the letter 'b', sticking a bee to each one.

Cross-curricular links
Stepping Stone
● Persevere in repeating some actions/attempts when developing a new skill. **(PD)**
Early Learning Goal
● Show awareness of space, of themselves and of others. **(PD)**

Buzzy bees

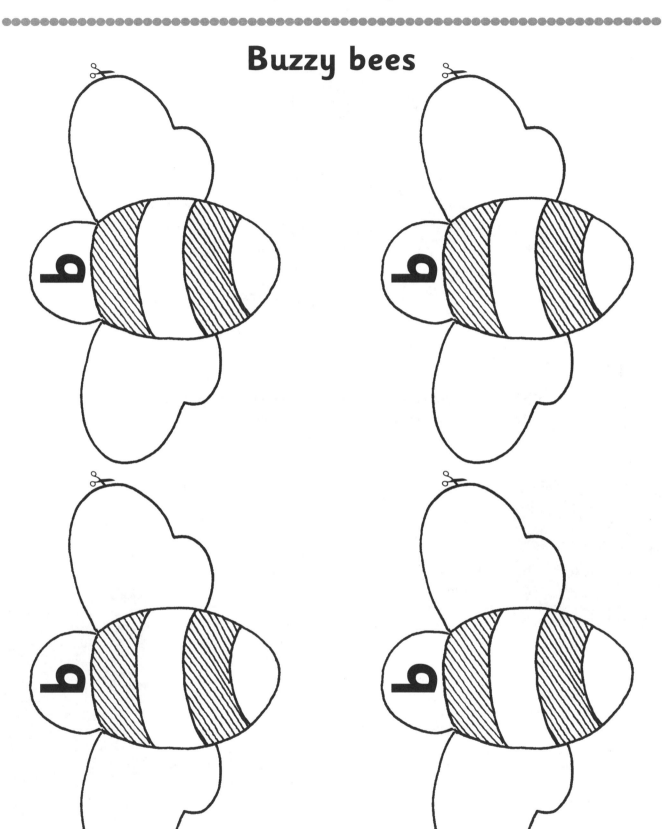

SCHOLASTIC
www.scholastic.co.uk

Silver snakes

Children explore silver, shiny items and have the opportunity to develop fine motor control by scrunching lengths of foil into snakes and bending these into letter shapes.

Early writers manipulate foil 'snakes' to make circles and trace around these with their fingers. **More confident writers** read and write words they associate with snakes and write captions.

What you need

Collection of silver coloured objects, such as chrome or stainless steel kitchenware, spoons, kitchen foil (folded and torn into lengths approximately 40 × 70cm); silver crayons; black paper; small lidded basket; picture of a snake; silver pen.

What to do

● Show the children the collection of silver items and let them handle and talk about the feel and reflective qualities of the objects. Prompt them to think and explore these qualities by asking questions such as: *Can you see your face in the spoon? What does a sheet of foil feel like when you run your hand over it? Does the foil look the same on both sides?*
● Give the group lengths of kitchen foil and ask the children to scrunch them up loosely

to make long silver snakes. Let them experiment in bending the foil to make snakes in different shapes. Draw some patterns and ask the children to see if they can make their snakes move into these patterns.
● Ask the children to try and write letters using the foil snakes by bending them into shape. Place these letters on to a piece of black paper and see which ones the group recognise.
● Make a simple interactive display with a picture of a snake and a lidded basket full of silver snakes made from foil. Show the children the picture and ask them what words they associate with snakes and write these on pieces of black

Learning objectives
Stepping Stones
● Manipulate objects with increasing control. **(CLL)**
● Use writing as a means of recording and communicating. **(CLL)**
Early Learning Goals
● Form recognisable letters, most of which are correctly formed. **(CLL)**
● Write their own names and other things such as labels and captions and begin to form simple sentences, sometimes using punctuation. **(CLL)**

paper in silver pen. The 'snake' words might include hiss, skin, long, body, bendy, sliding and tongue. Place these words in the lidded basket. The children should take a word, read it and write the word on the black paper by bending the silver foil snakes to form the letters. They can use silver crayons to write the word next to the foil snake.

Support and extension

● Younger children can make circles of different sizes using the foil snakes. Ask them to trace around the circles with their fingers, using an anticlockwise movement.

● Encourage older children to write captions about the snake in the picture on the display, using silver crayons on black paper.

Further activities

● If possible, show a video or DVD to illustrate a snake's natural habitat and the way it moves. (Copyright permitting.) Ask the children to describe this. Introduce the word 'slither' and invite the children to try moving along the floor like a snake.

● Show the children pictures of snakes and ask them to draw and cut out a long snake from black paper. Show them how to make circular and coiled patterns from lengths of scrunched up foil and glue these on to the snake outline to make a patterned skin.

Play links

● Give each child a short stick with a long ribbon tied to one end. Show them how to move the stick from side to side so that the ribbon looks like a snake. **(CD)**

● Encourage children to talk and play imaginatively by turning the sand tray or outdoor sandpit into a desert habitat for snakes. Include a variety of toy snakes, add large stones, pebbles and twigs, and let the children enjoy playing with this environment. Tell them that you are going to listen to them playing and write down some of the things they say. At the end of the session show them your writing and read out some of their comments, praising their ideas or use of words. **(CD)**

Home link

Invite parents and carers to provide kitchen foil for their children to try forming letters at home.

Cross-curricular links
Stepping Stone
● Manipulate materials to achieve a planned effect. **(PD)**
Early Learning Goal
● Handle tools, objects, construction and malleable materials safely and with increasing control. **(PD)**

Reasons for writing

Sandy signs

In this activity, children write with glue or glue sticks and make tactile letters by covering the glue with sand. They trace over the letters with their fingers, practising correct letter formation. They have the opportunity to talk about and read signs, and to write their own.

Early writers gain confidence in writing bold patterns and making marks using glue sticks, which glide easily over the page.
More confident writers experiment in writing their own signs in a fun way.

What you need
Dry sand; children's glue sticks; A4 or A3 cartridge paper to make signs.

What to do
● Before the session, write a letter 'c' on a piece of paper, using a glue stick. Cover the paper with sand, shaking off the excess to reveal the letter.
● Tell the children that you have written a letter that someone could read even in the dark. Ask them to close their eyes and run their fingers over the letter you have prepared and try to recognise it from the raised surface.
● Tell the children that you want them to imagine that they are on holiday at the seaside and have no pens or pencils. Ask them what kinds of signs they would expect to see. These might include 'Beach', 'Ice creams', 'Paddling pool', 'Open', 'Closed' or 'Fish and

Learning objectives
Stepping Stones
● Manipulate objects with increasing control. **(CLL)**
● Use writing as a means of recording and communicating. **(CLL)**
Early Learning Goals
● Form recognisable letters, most of which are correctly formed. **(CLL)**
● Write their own names and other things such as labels and captions. **(CLL)**

chips'. Write these words down and read them together.

● Tell the children that you want them to write some seaside signs but all they have got to write with is a glue stick and sand.

● Depending on the stage they are at, either let the children write their own signs with the glue sticks, copy your writing or write the signs for them to trace over. When they have finished the writing, the children can cover the page in sand and shake off the excess, revealing their signs.

● Check that the children are forming letters correctly by asking them to trace over the sandy letters with their fingers. If they are not, put a dot where they should begin to form the letter and ask them to use this as a starting point.

Support and extension

● Ask younger children to make wavy, zigzag or dotty patterns using the glue stick and cover these with sand.

● Older children can work together to write each letter of the alphabet in glue and sand. When the letters are dry, ask the children to cut them out. Mount the letters on a board at child height so that they can trace around them with their fingers.

Further activities

● Ask the children to write their names using materials such as coloured sand or fine gravel to create different effects.

● Paint giant letters and writing patterns working from left to right, using PVA glue and thick brushes on large sheets of cartridge paper. Cover with sand and shake off the excess.

Play link

Set up an area where children can play with dry sand and add water to it. Provide buckets, spades, spoons, plastic tubs; bottles, sieves and watering cans. Through play, let the children discover the differences between the properties of wet and dry sand. Will wet sand run through the sieve? Can you make a sandcastle from dry sand? Is wet sand the same colour as dry sand? **(KUW)**

Home link

Ask parents and carers to read signs with their children on their way to and from the setting.

Cross-curricular links
Stepping Stone
● Begin to try out a range of tools and techniques safely. **(KUW)**
Early Learning Goal
● Select the tools and techniques they need to shape, assemble and join materials they are using. **(KUW)**

The longest list

This activity is introduced through the picture book, *Don't Forget the Bacon* by Pat Hutchins (Red Fox). The children think of items they want to buy from the supermarket and add them to a giant shopping list by dipping a sponge into paint and writing the words on a long roll of paper.

Early writers either dictate their list and write over the adult's writing, or use word lists to help them write their own lists. **More confident writers** make a list and also write sentences about an imaginary person.

What you need

Copy of *Don't Forget the Bacon* by Pat Hutchins (Red Fox); long roll of paper; pieces of sponge; ready-mixed paints in plastic tubs; aprons.

What to do

● Outside, or in a separate area of the setting out of sight, roll out a long length of paper and provide tubs of paint and small sponges for the children to use.
● Read the story *Don't Forget the Bacon* by Pat Hutchins. Talk about the items which the boy had to buy when he went to the shops and how he mixed up the things he needed. Ask the children if they can think of a way that would have helped him to

remember what to buy when he went shopping. Introduce the idea of writing a list.
● Invite the children to tell you things which they could buy on a visit to a supermarket. Remind them of the different sections in the shop they could visit, such as fruit and vegetables, meat, bread, cereals, baking and frozen food. List their suggestions, re-reading the list to them as you make it. As the list gets longer, tell the children that you are running out of space but you have a piece of paper that they can use to write the longest list they have ever seen.
● Show them the prepared paper and paints. Provide them with aprons and let

Learning objectives
Stepping Stone
● Use writing as a means of recording and communicating. **(CLL)**
Early Learning Goal
● Attempt writing for different purposes, using features of different forms such as lists. **(CLL)**

the children arrange themselves along the length of the paper and start dipping the sponges into the paint and writing the list. They may like to make drawings of some of the items as they go along.

● When the list is completed, read and discuss it together. When it is dry, roll it up and let the children take it to show another group of children, explaining what they have done and reading words from the list.

Support and extension

● Younger children may find it easier to write their own lists on large sheets of paper. You can act as scribe and the children write over your writing or they read and copy words from a word list.

● Ask older children to imagine that they have found the long list when out shopping. Who do they think might have written such an enormous list? Is it someone very, very big? Is it someone very, very hungry? Or someone with lots of children? Ask them to draw a picture of the person who wrote the list and write a few sentences about that person.

Further activities

● Ask the children to decide together which five items they would like to buy for their snacks that week. Talk about healthy options such as different types of fruit. Write the list as the children make their decisions. If possible make arrangements to visit a nearby shop where the children can take the list and buy the items.

● Gather together about ten items which could be bought from a supermarket and place on a tray. Ask the children to look carefully at the items and try to remember what they are. Cover them with a cloth and ask the children to name them.

Play link

Provide a shopping basket, real grocery items such as small tins of food and empty packets, a purse and coins, shopping list pad and pen to encourage role play. **(CD)**

Home link

Suggest that parents or carers let their children help to write a list before they go shopping. As they shop, they can cross the items off.

Cross-curricular links
Stepping Stone
● Demonstrate increasing skill and control in the use of mark-making implements. **(PD)**
Early Learning Goal
● Handle tools, objects, construction and malleable materials safely and with increasing control. **(PD)**

Glitter writing

This Christmas activity is appealing to children who love to use copious amounts of glitter. They examine shiny fabrics, foils and decorations. They describe and draw Christmas tree decorations to make into a book and write with glue, covering the letters with glitter.

Early writers cut out shapes from foil and use a glue stick to draw patterns which they cover with glitter.
More confident writers write adjectives describing stars in their own star-shaped books.

What you need
Basket or box; decorated Christmas tree with lights; lengths of shiny fabrics; glitter; glue; coloured foil; aluminium foil; shiny paper; assortment of shiny Christmas tree decorations (check these are shatter-proof and safe for children to handle); shiny ribbon; hole-punch.

What to do
● Make up a basket or box of the items above and encourage the children to handle the fabrics, baubles and foils, describing their texture and appearance using words such as 'smooth', 'shiny', 'glittery' and 'sparkly'. Give the children the opportunity to wrap themselves in the fabrics, to drape and explore their qualities.

Ask questions to extend their thinking such as: *Do you think the decorations will still be shiny if it is dark?* Examine the collection in a darkened area and listen to the children's comments. Ask further questions such as: *If they are not shiny now, what do we need to make them shiny again?*
● Look at the decorated Christmas tree with and without the lights switched on. Talk about the way that the decorations shine when the tree is lit up. Suggest to the children that you make a shiny book together to show to their parents or carers, showing different tree decorations such as stars, bells or icicles.

Learning objectives
Stepping Stones
● Draw and paint, sometimes giving meanings to marks. **(CLL)**
● Hear and say the initial sound in words and know which letters represent some of the sounds. **(CLL)**
Early Learning Goals
● Write their own names and other things such as labels and captions. **(CLL)**
● Hear and say initial and final sounds in words. **(CLL)**

● Ask the children to tell you words that describe the decorations. Say these words together, encouraging the children to enjoy the sounds which make up the words. Sound the words out together, listening to the separate syllables.

● Provide each child with a piece of coloured foil approximately 20 × 15cm. Explain that in order to make the book extra shiny they are going to use glitter for their writing and drawing. Ask them to draw a Christmas decoration on to the piece of foil using a glue stick and then to write a word to describe it, such as 'shiny' or 'sparkly'. Sprinkle glitter over the paper and shake off the excess, revealing the glittery drawing and writing. When dry, put the sheets together, punch holes in one side and tie shiny ribbon through the holes to make a book to share.

Support and extension

● Younger children can cut out shapes from coloured foil and decorate with patterns using the glue stick.

● Encourage older children to make individual books by cutting out star shapes and writing adjectives to describe stars such as 'shiny', 'glittery', 'sparkly' or 'twinkling' on each one. Staple the stars together to make a simple book.

Further activity

● Make a Christmas dictionary using a simple Christmas tree shaped book with 26 pages and a front cover. Staple the sheets together and write the letters of the alphabet on each page in glitter writing. Ask the children to think of words associated with Christmas, beginning with each letter of the alphabet and to write these using gold or silver pens on the appropriate page in the book. Decorate the cover with gold, silver and glitter.

Play link

Display a small Christmas tree (a real one if possible) and a box of Christmas decorations for children to decorate their own tree.

Home link

Suggest that parents or carers allow time for their children to look and wonder at the wide variety of Christmas decorations available.

Cross-curricular links
Stepping Stone
● Begin to describe the texture of things. **(CD)**
Early Learning Goal
● Explore colour, texture, shape, form and space in two or three dimensions. **(CD)**

Autumn leaves

Children explore and use their senses when playing with fallen leaves. They think of words to describe the texture and colours of the leaves, and use the leaves to write letters and words, inside and outside. They read and write the names of colours to describe autumn.

Early writers trace over words with their fingers and glue leaves in place to form words.
More confident writers make a tree of words associated with their walk.

What you need

A dry day in autumn; a safe area where different coloured leaves have fallen from the trees; plastic bags for collecting leaves; large sheets of paper; glue; ready-mixed paints (the colours of autumn leaves); large paintbrushes; crayons; digital camera; hand-washing facilities; basket.

What to do

● Plan this activity carefully, completing the necessary risk assessments and safety procedures beforehand. Choose an area where the children will be safe to play and make sure there is no animal faeces. Give the children time to run about and enjoy playing in the leaves, kicking them and listening to the rustling sounds.

● Gather the children together and ask them to examine the leaves and tell you about the colours and textures. How many different colours can they see? Is a leaf just one plain colour? Can they see the veins in the leaf? What happens when they scrunch a leaf in their hands? Are all of the leaves the same shape?

● Invite the children to help you write giant letters or words on the ground using armfuls of leaves. Ask the children if they think these letters will stay in place. What might move them away? Take photos of the leaves to use as part of a display later.

● Give each child a bag and ask them to collect leaves to take back to the setting. On your return, tip

Learning objectives
Stepping Stone
● Use writing as a means of recording and communication. **(CLL)**
Early Learning Goal
● Attempt writing for different purposes, using features of different forms such as lists, stories and instructions. **(CLL)**

out the bags of leaves and tell the children that you want them to sort the leaves by colour.

● When they have finished, ask the children to work in pairs choosing leaves from one of the 'colour' piles. Invite them to write the colour name on a large sheet of paper using the leaves of the appropriate colour to form the letters. Glue the leaves on to the paper. Ask the children to read aloud the words that they have written to the rest of the group and to tell you the initial sounds of the words.

● Discuss the reasons why they need to wash their hands thoroughly after playing with the leaves. Then, ask the children to choose the appropriate colours from the ready-mixed paints and to write the colour words on their sheets using paint and brushes, and then again using the appropriate coloured crayon. Fill a basket with leaves and display their work around it, including the photographs of the leaf words from outside.

Support and extension

● Write the colour word for younger children to trace over with their fingers and then ask them to glue leaves on top of the letters to make the word.

● Ask older children to draw and paint a large tree and cut out leaf shapes from coloured paper. Using pens in autumn colours, ask the children to write words associated with their walk, such as 'tree', 'leaf', 'branch', 'windy', 'crunchy' or 'rustling'.

Further activities

● Paint one side of a leaf, and make large leaf print letters by pressing the leaf on to paper.

● Act as scribe and compose a poem together about leaves, using words to describe their appearance, texture and the sounds they make underfoot or as they blow in the wind.

Play link

Set up a table with containers of leaves, conkers, dried seed heads, glue and large sheets of paper. Encourage the children to experiment freely in making their own collages. **(CD)**

Home link

Suggest that parents and carers talk with their children about the signs of autumn and changing colours as they walk to the setting.

Cross-curricular links
Stepping Stone
● Show curiosity, observe and manipulate objects. **(KUW)**
Early Learning Goal
● Investigate objects and materials by using all of their senses as appropriate. **(KUW)**

Treasure box

In this activity, the children look inside a treasure box and find that when they hold each item there are unexpected results. The aim is to encourage children to think about and experience feelings which they can then talk about and will motivate them to write.

Early writers put their thoughts into words which they dictate to an adult. They write over or below the writing.
More confident writers write labels and sentences about what they have experienced.

What you need
Small treasure box; small teddy bear; gold star (a Christmas decoration or star made from card); spring; pebble, gold pens; pieces of card; the following four messages written in gold on pieces of card and placed in an envelope: *When you hold* [one of the items] *you will want to … jump for joy, …smile at a friend, …say something kind, …hug a friend.*

What to do
● Before the session, place the small teddy bear, gold star, spring, pebble and so on inside the treasure box.
● Invite the children to sit in a circle and place the treasure box in the middle. Ask them to speculate about what might be inside it. If it is treasure, what sort of treasure? Where did it come from? Who does it belong to? Build up the suspense and encourage the children to use their imaginations. If you have a key, slowly and ceremoniously unlock the box to reveal the contents.
● Examine the items inside the box. Is this what they had expected to see? Does it look like treasure? Wait a minute – there is something else! Show the children the envelope. Ask one of them to open it to reveal the cards.

Learning objectives
Stepping Stones
● Begin to use talk to pretend imaginary situations. **(CLL)**
● Use writing as a means of recording and communicating. **(CLL)**
Early Learning Goals
● Use talk to organise, sequence and clarify thinking, ideas, feelings and events. **(CLL)**
● Write their own names and other things such as labels and captions and begin to form simple sentences, sometimes using punctuation. **(CLL)**

● Read the first card out loud, for example 'When you hold the pink stone you will want to jump for joy'. Pass the pebble to another adult who obliges by jumping for joy. How could that happen? Is it magic? Pass the pebble to a child to see if it works for them too. If it does not, hold the pebble yourself and jump in the air. After passing it to other children who want to join in, repeat the procedure with all of the other items.

● When the children have had time to try out, talk about and play with the items, ask them if they have enjoyed playing with the things they have found. Tell them that you noticed that they looked happy – smiling and jumping for joy – and they made other children feel happy too by saying kind things and giving hugs. Although the objects did not look like the treasure they had expected – could they have been treasure after all?

● Ask the children to choose one more item which could be added to the box. What would it make them want to do? Suggestions could include *run and jump, sing and dance*, or *find a new friend*. Ask them to find an object and using a gold pen, write and illustrate their own card to add to the treasure box.

Support and extension

● Encourage younger children to dictate what they want to write and overwrite or copy-write using a gold pen.

● Older children can draw and label the treasure box and its contents, and write sentences about what happened when they held one of the items.

Further activity

● Provide small paper bags for the children to decorate and fill with treasure such as coloured stones, shells, beads or necklaces. Add tags for the children to write their names.

Play link

Set up a table with shiny papers, beads, string, scissors and glue so that children can make their own treasure. **(CD)**

Home link

Make a display of the children's work in the setting so that they can show their parents and carers and explain what they have been doing.

Cross-curricular links
Stepping Stone
● Display high levels of involvement in activities. **(PSED)**
Early Learning Goal
● Be confident to try new activities, initiate ideas and speak in a familiar group. **(PSED)**

Making games

In this activity the children create a simple outdoor dice game by choosing and writing instructions on a play surface for others to follow.

What you need
Outside play area; chalks; large dice; chalkboards; 'What shall I do?' photocopiable page 35.

What to do
● Before starting this activity, play warm-up games outside, then tell the children that you are going to give instructions and they must listen carefully and follow the instruction straight away. Call out words such as 'run', 'clap', 'stamp', 'skip', 'jump' and 'hop', to get children moving and enjoying themselves.

● Explain to the children that you want them to make a playground game that everyone can enjoy. Draw six 50 × 50cm squares in a line. Ask the children to use chalk to write the numbers one to six in order, on the squares.

● Call out the commands you used earlier and ask the children to write the words on their chalkboards. Write the words on your own chalkboard and ask them to check their spelling against yours.

● Ask the children to choose six instructions to use in the game and then to write one of these words in each of the squares on the ground. To play the game, the children take it in turns to throw a large dice, read the number on the dice and find the appropriate square. They read the word in the square and follow the instruction. If they throw a six they have another turn.

● Play this activity indoors to reinforce learning using the 'What shall I do?' photocopiable page 35. It can be used as a five minute lesson at the start or end of the day. Copy the photocopiable sheet on to card and invite the children to play the game. Ask them to trace their finger over the words on the cards before they begin to play. Then, cut out the cards and turn them face down. Playing in pairs, each child should then pick a card and do what it says.

Support and extension
● Invite younger children to write the initial sound in a word while an adult helps them complete it.
● Older children can extend their instructions when writing, such as, 'Stamp your feet!', 'Clap five times' and so on.

Further activity
● Provide a box of balls outside and ask the children to use chalk to write instructions such as, 'Throw a ball', 'Bounce a ball', 'Roll a ball', on the play surface near the box.

Home link
Suggest that the children read the words from the play area to their parents and carers, showing them how well they can perform each action.

What shall I do?

hop	skip
jump	run
clap	stamp

Crosswords

In this activity, children listen to and enjoy the sounds of rhyming CVC words and write letters or words.

What you need

'Crosswords' photocopiable page 37 enlarged to A3 and copied on to card; thick felt-tipped pens; whiteboard and pen.

What to do

● Read traditional poems and nursery rhymes to the group and ask the children to listen for the words that rhyme. Leave a gap for the children to tell you the missing rhyming word, for example, use 'Hickory Dickory Dock':

Hickory Dickory Dock
The mouse ran up the…

● Give the children time to enjoy hearing the rhyming sounds and to tell you other words from the same rhyming family, such as 'sock', 'lock' and 'rock', or encourage them to play with words and make up their own words such as 'bock' or 'gock'.

● Choose a family of CVC rhyming words, such as 'can', 'fan', 'man', 'pan' and 'ran'. Ask the children to listen for the initial, middle and final sounds in the words and sound the letters as you write them on a whiteboard. Play games to encourage the children to choose the appropriate word, for example: *It has a handle. I cook potatoes in it. What is it?* Ask them to write the word, or the first letter of the word, in the air.

● Enlarge the photocopiable sheet on to A3 card and cut out the letter cards. Show the

> **Early writers** sing rhyming songs, link sounds to letters and paint the letters.
> **More confident writers** list rhyming CVC words.

children one of the sets of letters from the photocopiable sheet and ask them to make two CVC rhyming words in a very simple crossword shape. Tell them to make the horizontal word first. Children can also use thick felt-tipped pens to write their own letters on the blank cards to make rhyming CVC words.

Support and extension

● Encourage younger children to sing songs, listening for and repeating the rhyming words. They can paint the first letter of the word or attempt the whole word.

● Older children can use glitter pens to write lists of rhyming CVC words to read aloud and share in a group.

Further activities

● Write words on cards from three rhyming CVC families such as: 'can', 'van', 'man'; 'hat', 'mat', 'cat'; 'rub', 'dub', 'tub'. Mix these up and ask the children sort them into rhyming families.

● Put the cards face down on the table. Ask children to turn over one card, read it and use a glitter pen to write another rhyming word from the same family.

Home link

Suggest that parents and carers encourage their children to listen for rhyming words when they sing or read to them.

> ## Learning objectives
> **Stepping Stones**
> ● Continue a rhyming string. **(CLL)**
> ● Use writing as a means of recording and communicating. **(CLL)**
> **Early Learning Goals**
> ● Hear and say initial and final sounds in words, and short vowel sounds within words. **(CLL)**
> ● Attempt writing for different purposes, using features of different forms such as lists. **(CLL)**

> ## Cross-curricular links
> **Stepping Stones**
> ● Sing a few simple, familiar songs. **(CD)**
> ● Begin to build a repertoire of songs. **(CD)**
> **Early Learning Goal**
> ● Recognise and explore how sounds can be changed, sing simple songs from memory, recognise repeated sounds and sound patterns and match movements to music. **(CD)**

Crosswords

```
      m
p  a  n
   n

   h
t  o  p
   p
```

```
      s
b  i  t
   t
```

Drive along

In this activity, children explore their local area and record their findings in simple pictorial maps. They experiment in mark-making and writing, using toy cars which have had their wheels dipped in paint.

What you need
Safe, local area; small toy cars; clean margarine tubs containing ready-mixed paints (only fill as deep as the axles on the cars you are using); large sheet of paper approximately 1.5 × 1m; digital camera; 'Picture map' photocopiable page 39 enlarged to A3; thick felt-tipped pens.

Early writers experiment with mark-making.
More confident writers make lists and labels.

What to do
● Arrange a walk around the local area, carrying out the necessary risk assessments and safety procedures. On the walk, ask the children to look out for different features, such as houses, shops, churches and play areas. Take photographs of these to use as talking points on your return.
● After the walk, show the children the photocopiable sheet and ask them to talk about the features they can see. Explain that that they are going to make a picture map of their own, to include some of the things they have seen on their walk. Start by drawing the roads. Demonstrate how to dip the toy cars into the paint and draw lines to represent roads. Let the children experiment with drawing patterns and writing their names using the cars before asking them to draw the roads on the large sheet of paper in this way.
● Make a list together of the different features they have seen on their walk. Ask the children to draw and paint some of these features, such as houses, shops, trees, church, pond, play area and school on to the map. Using thick felt-tipped pens, ask the children to refer to the list and write labels naming these features on the map.

Support and extension
● Younger children can make 3D maps by dipping the car wheels in paint and drawing roads using wavy, zigzag or curved lines. When dry, add small-world items such as buildings, road signs, people, vehicles and animals.
● Encourage older children to talk about the features they like and dislike in the local area and list these inside smiley or sad faces.

Further activity
● Draw a very simple map showing the roads around the setting. Ask the children to place the photographs in the appropriate locations. Set the children problems to solve using the cars, such as: *Draw a red route from the school to the park. Draw a blue route from the fish and chip shop to the library. How can I get from the swimming pool to the church?*

Home link
Suggest to parents and carers that they encourage their children to talk about features of the area in which they live. Can they name the types of buildings? Which ones do they like? Why?

Picture map

Raindrops

In this activity children are encouraged to listen carefully to sounds made by musical instruments and to link the sounds they hear at the beginning, middle and ends of words to the letters that they write.

Early writers paint on to wet paper the letters that they hear at the beginning of words. **More confident writers** make up their own sentences and write them using fine brushes and ink.

What you need

Plastic bucket containing a small pair of Wellington boots, umbrella, plastic duck, triangle and metal beater, and rainstick; individual whiteboards and pens; strips of paper; raindrops (made from card); laminator; blue ink; brushes; beach towel.

What to do

● Present the children with the bucket and ask them to take out an item and name it. Put all of the items together and ask the children what the items all have in common, giving their reasons. Elicit the response, 'water'. But what about the triangle and beater? What have they to do with water?
● Pick up the triangle and strike it lightly to

sound like water dripping. Ask the children if the sound reminds them of any particular weather. Let them experiment in making sounds using the triangle and rainstick and talk about the sounds.
● Ask the children to tell you the name of each item in the bucket and the first sound they hear in that word. Can they also hear the middle and last sounds? Ask them to write the first sound on their individual whiteboards and then try to write the rest of the word. Read and praise their attempts and write the word on to a raindrop shape made from card. Laminate the raindrops and place in the bucket.
● Ask each child to take a

Learning objectives
Stepping Stone
● Hear and say the initial sounds in words and know which letters represent some of the sounds. **(CLL)**
Early Learning Goal
● Use their phonic knowledge to write simple regular words and make phonetically plausible attempts at more complex words. **(CLL)**

raindrop from the bucket and to read the word, telling you something about it in a sentence, such as, 'Boots keep my feet dry.' 'The duck swims in water.' Some children may be able write their sentences on the strips of paper using fine brushes and diluted blue ink to give a watery effect. Laminate the strips.
● Display the contents of the bucket on a beach towel outdoors, along with the laminated raindrops and watery sentences in a bucket of water. Give the children time to play with these, reading the words and sentences as they do so.

Support and extension
● Invite younger children to paint the first letter of the words on to wet paper and see the effect.
● Encourage older children to listen to the sounds of water dripping from a tap, rain against a window, or pebbles dropping into a bowl of water and list words to describe the sounds.

Further activity
● Teach the children this poem. Say it together when you are out enjoying a walk on a wet day. Let the children enjoy the experience of walking in puddles and listening to the sounds of rain.

Welly Walking

Tip, tap.
Tip, tap.
Can you hear the rain?

Drip, drop.
Splitter, splot.
Here it comes again.

Welly walking,
Clump, clump, clump.

Welly walking,
Let's all jump.

Welly walking,
Splish, splosh, splash.

Here comes thunder.
Quick let's dash.

By Julie Boden

Play link
Sing rain songs such as 'Rain, rain, go away' and 'I hear the thunder' (Traditional). Provide a variety of musical instruments to encourage children to experiment in making the sounds of rain and water. **(CD)**

Home link
Give the children a copy of the poem to take home so that parents and carers can share the poem with their children when walking in the rain.

Cross-curricular links
Stepping Stones
● Show an interest in the way musical instruments sound. **(CD)**
● Explore the different sounds of instruments. **(CD)**
Early Learning Goal
● Recognise and explore how sounds can be changed, sing simple songs from memory, recognise repeated sounds and sound patterns and match movements to music. **(CD)**

At the seaside

This activity is ideal for a warm summer's day. The children go on an imaginary visit to the seaside and talk about their own experiences of the seaside. They play in the water and sand, and list words or draw pictures by writing with a stick in wet sand.

Early writers have the opportunity to enjoy mark-making in a different context.
More confident writers write lists and make labels.

What you need

Large sand tray or, if possible, an outside area covered in clean play sand; paddling pool; buckets and spades; rug; picnic basket filled with snacks and drinks; digital camera; sunhats; short sticks or twigs; adult helpers; 'I can see the sea!' photocopiable page 44.

What to do

● Read the story 'I can see the sea!', inserting your name and the children's names in the appropriate places. Give the children time to talk about their experiences of the seaside and what they enjoy most about it. Collect items which they might take on a day out to the seaside, such as buckets and spades, a rug to sit on and a picnic basket. Prepare the paddling pool,

sand tray or sand area in an area where the children would not usually use them. Provide shade if it is a hot day.

● Tell the children that you are all going on a visit like the one in the story. Pack the items you need for a day out and take snacks and drinks in the picnic basket, ensuring to check with parents and carers first for any food allergies or dietary requirements. Remind the children about the importance of wearing a hat and talk to them about sun safety.

● Build up the excitement and set off on the journey, eventually arriving at the

Learning objectives
Stepping Stones
● Ascribe meaning to marks. **(CLL)**
● Use writing as a means of recording and communicating. **(CLL)**
● Use talk, actions and objects to recall and relive past experiences. **(CLL)**
Early Learning Goals
● Attempt writing for different purposes, using features of different forms such as lists, stories and instructions. **(CLL)**
● Use talk to organise, sequence and clarify thinking, ideas, feelings and events. **(CLL)**

sand and water area. Give the children time to enjoy playing in the sand and paddling in the pool, ensuring that they are well-supervised at all times. Encourage the children to imagine that they really are at the seaside by your comments such as, 'Mind the waves!', 'Can you hear the seagulls?', 'Look at that crab!', 'There's a ship out at sea!'.

● Gather the children together for their snack and drink and ask them to tell you which things they see at the seaside. Ask them to make a list of these things by writing with a stick in the wet sand in whichever way is appropriate to them, either writing the word, the first letter of each word or by making marks. Take a photograph of each child's list as a record of their seaside visit.

Support and extension
● Write the words lightly in the sand for younger children to trace over or write the words on a large sheet of paper for them to read and copy.
● Older children can look at the photographs of their lists of words and paint

them again on a large piece of sand-coloured paper, drawing a picture of each item next to the word.

Further activity
● Make a 'For Sale' sign and collect together items such as the buckets, spades, rug and picnic basket used in the main activity. Tell the children that these items are for sale in a seaside shop. Make an illustrated wordlist of the items in order to support the children's writing and ask them to write labels with prices for each item.

Play link
Provide a bucketful of shells for the children to handle, sort and make into patterns or pictures. **(CD)**

Home link
Suggest that parents and carers talk to their children about holidays or days out they have enjoyed together – where they went, what they did or saw.

Cross-curricular links
Stepping Stone
● Show an interest in the world in which they live. **(KUW)**
Early Learning Goal
● Observe, find out about and identify features in the place they live and the natural world. **(KUW)**

I can see the sea!

The children of _____ school just could not wait. _____ and _____ were jumping up and down with excitement.

'We are going to the seaside today, aren't we?' asked _____.

'Yes, yes, we are', said M_____. 'It is today, but you must all line up quietly so that we can check we have got everything. Now, let me look at my list. Have we got the buckets, spades, a rug and the picnic basket?'

'Yes! Yes!' shouted everyone, all keen to get started.

'It's sunny out there today, so make sure you've all got your hats on.'

M_____ quickly checked that everyone was wearing a hat and at last they set off. The adventure had begun. They walked and talked and laughed and giggled.

_____s legs suddenly felt tired and she was feeling hot and thirsty. 'Are we nearly there yet?' she asked

'Yes, nearly there' said M_____ 'Keep your eyes open for the sea – it's not much further.'

The children grew more excited. 'I can see the sea! It's really blue!' shouted

_____.

'So can I!' shouted _____.

The children ran to the beach. They played in the sand, splashed in the rock pools and let the wind blow against their faces. _____ looked up into the sky and saw seagulls overhead. _____ looked out to sea and saw a tiny ship far in the distance. _____ looked into a rock pool and saw a crab scuttling away behind a rock.

They all picked up sticks left by the sea and drew pictures and wrote their names in the wet sand. M _____ took photos as she said that the sea would wash away their drawings.

'I think this is the best day, ever!' said _____, as the cool water in the rock pool tickled his toes.

Writing stories and poems

The Gingerbread Man

In this activity the children make their own gingerbread man from play dough to incorporate into the interactive story page.

What you need

The Gingerbread Man illustrated by Anja Reiger (*First Favourite Tales* series, Ladybird Books); modelling material such as play dough; 'The Gingerbread Man' photocopiable page 46 enlarged to A3 and 'The Gingerbread Man: Templates' photocopiable page 47; scissors; glue.

Learning objectives
Stepping Stone
● Describe main story settings, events and principal characters. **(CLL)**
Early Learning Goal
● Sustain attentive listening, responding to what they have heard by relevant comments, questions or actions. **(CLL)**

What to do

● Read the story of *The Gingerbread Man*, encouraging the children to join in.
● Read the story again, this time with the children role playing the characters. Ask them to name and describe the characters in the story. Which character do they like and why? How do they feel about the fox? Did they think that he would eat the gingerbread man?
● Talk about the different settings in the story – the kitchen, the road and the river and encourage them to retell the main events in the correct order.
● Show the children 'The Gingerbread Man' photocopiable page 46 and ask them what is missing from each picture. Explain that they are going to make the missing gingerbread man from play dough for their story page. The gingerbread men should be 7–8cm tall (see the template on page 47).

Early writers paint a scene from the story, adding their own play dough gingerbread man to the picture.
More confident writers use a computer to write sentences, telling the story.

● Let the children decide where the gingerbread man should go on each picture. Cut out the speech bubbles from page 47 and read these together before sticking them in the correct places and telling the story together.

Support and extension

● Younger children can paint a scene from the story and incorporate their play dough gingerbread man into the picture.
● Encourage older children to use a computer to write and print a sentence to add below each picture.

Further activity

● With the children, find a gingerbread biscuit recipe from a cookery book or by using the internet. Make, bake and eat gingerbread men biscuits, ensuring to check with parents and carers first for any food allergies or dietary requirements. Remind the children about the importance of following hygiene and safety rules when baking.

Home link

Invite the children to take home a gingerbread man which they have baked and retell the story of *The Gingerbread Man* to a parent or carer.

Cross-curricular links
Stepping Stone
● Manipulate materials to achieve a planned effect. **(PD)**
Early Learning Goal
● Handle tools, objects, construction and malleable materials safely and with increasing control. **(PD)**

The Gingerbread Man

SCHOLASTIC

www.scholastic.co.uk

The Gingerbread Man: Templates

I'll help you cross the river!

You can't catch me I'm the Gingerbread Man!

Stop, Gingerbread Man!

Yummy!

Story wall

Listening to and enacting a story are the starting points for this writing activity. The children have the opportunity to take part in role play, talk about the story and describe the characters so that they begin to understand what a story is and feel motivated to write. The children write freely on a large scale.

Early writers have the opportunity to draw and write using large shoulder movements. **More confident writers** retell a story in simple sentences or by writing comments in speech or thought bubbles.

What you need
Roll or large sheets of paper; finger-paints; a favourite story.

What to do
● At child height, attach the roll or large sheets of paper to a wall either inside or outside. The area covered should be at least one and a half metres long and one metre high to allow children the freedom to work on a large scale.

● Read a favourite story to the children and ask them to role play the characters while you are reading. Ask the children to retell the story to another group of children, making sure that they have the events in the correct sequence. The sequencing of events in the story gives the opportunity to ask questions using the language of time, for example, *What happened next? Did Auntie Duck arrive before Granda Duck? Who arrived after Granda Duck?* and so on.

● Talk about the characters and what they are like. Ask the children to work together to draw pictures of the characters and write simple sentences about the events in the story using finger-paints on a large sheet of paper. They can share the story with their parents or carers at the end of the session. Encourage the children to

Learning objectives
Stepping Stones
● Ascribe meanings to marks. **(CLL)**
● Begin to be aware of the way stories are structured. **(CLL)**
Early Learning Goals
● Attempt writing for different purposes, using features of different forms such as lists, stories and instructions. **(CLL)**
● Retell narratives in the correct sequence, drawing on language patterns of stories. **(CLL)**

work on a large scale mixing writing and drawings. When the drawings are completed, talk to the children about what they think the characters might be saying. Depending on the children's level, you may like to add speech or thought bubbles to extend their writing.

Support and extension

● Ask younger children to draw one of the characters from the story, and write the character's name or attempt to write the first sound in the character's name using giant letters.

● Older children can make a record of the story showing the main events in the correct sequence, using one large sheet of paper for each event. Number the sheets. Read this giant book together at the end of the session.

Further activity

● Make a zigzag book of 'Who's who?' in favourite stories, to keep in the book corner for everyone to share. The children can write the title and author's name on the front cover of the zigzag book and draw and name each of the characters in the story on the following pages.

Play link

Make a role-play box which includes a story book, artefacts and dressing up clothes appropriate to the story. Encourage the children to cooperate with each other as they take on the roles of the characters and bring the story to life. Add a box of small booklets and a variety of crayons to encourage spontaneous attempts at writing. **(CLL)**

Home link

Suggest to parents or carers that after sharing stories with their children, they talk about the characters and retell the story together.

Cross-curricular links

Stepping Stone
● Work creatively on a large or small scale. **(CD)**
Early Learning Goal
● Explore colour, texture, shape, form and space in two or three dimensions. **(CD)**

Whose footprints?

In this activity, the children find some tiny footprints and spilled paint. The practitioner creates the scenes and the children use their imaginations as they become part of the story. They create and retell the story in photographs.

Early writers begin to understand the concept of a story.
More confident writers work imaginatively, retelling a story in the correct sequence.

What you need
Paint in pot; saucer; milk; cushion or fabric; basket or box; toy cat; digital camera.

What to do
● Before the children arrive, paint cat-like footprints on a table and leave a paint pot tipped on its side with paint spilled. As the children come in, show them the footprints and spilled paint. Who do they think has been in the room? Would a person make such small footprints? If not, who could it be? Take a photo of the children examining the footprints. (Ensure you get parents' or carers' permission before taking photographs.)
● Determine that the footprints were made by a small animal, probably a cat. Ask the children if they think the cat is still in the

room. Let them start searching in case it is. Take another two photos of the children searching under and on top of things.
● As the cat has gone, ask the children to suggest ways to find it. Do they think it might be hungry? If they left out a saucer of milk might it come and drink it? Ask the children to pour some milk into a saucer at the end of the session and take another photo as they do so.
● When the children return to the room, they find that the milk has gone, but there is still no sign of the cat. Take a photo of the empty saucer.
● The children realise that the cat has been while they were out of the room. How could they attract the cat back again? What else

Learning objectives
Stepping Stone
● Begin to be aware of the way stories are structured. **(CLL)**
Early Learning Goal
● Show an understanding of the elements of stories, such as main character, sequence of events and openings. **(CLL)**

might it need? What if it is tired? What could they leave out for it to sleep in?

● Line a basket or box with a cushion or soft fabric. Put out another saucer of milk and take the children outside or into another room. Take a photo of the bed and milk.

● When you return later, open the door slowly and quietly and peep in so that the cat, if it is there, won't be frightened. Open the door to reveal the milk gone and the cat curled up in the basket. Take a photo of the empty saucer and the toy cat asleep.

● Let the children pick up the cat and discover it is not real. Take a photo of the children stroking the cat. If it is not real, how did it get there? How did it drink the milk and knock over the paint and leave footprints? Ask the children to talk to a partner about their theories and then come back together and discuss as a group.

● Print the photographs and make them into a zigzag book or a slideshow on the computer. The children can retell the story using the pictures. Alternatively they can tell the story and you act as scribe, reading the story back to them. They have created a story. They are authors.

Support and extension
● Invite younger children to share the book with an adult, talking about the pictures.
● Encourage older children to write captions for the photographs, using the computer.

Further activity
● Keep the talk and speculation going by adding new twists to engage the children, such as telling them that you saw the cat in the garden or getting on a bus. Have the children seen it anywhere?

Play link
Set up a vet's bag so that the children can look after the cat if it is ill. **(CD)**

Home link
Put the cat in a basket with a saucer and brush. Ask the children if they would like to take it home (in turn) and look after it for a night.

Cross-curricular links
Stepping Stone
● Play alongside other children who are engaged in the same theme. **(CD)**
Early Learning Goal
● Use their imagination in art and design, music, dance, imaginative and role play and stories. **(CD)**

Big puzzles

In this activity, the children put the events of a traditional story in the correct sequence by making a story puzzle. They write words or sentences using paints or pens.

What you need

A copy of *The Enormous Turnip* illustrated by Jan Lewis (*First Favourite Tales* series, Ladybird Books); 'Story puzzle' photocopiable page 53 enlarged to A3; paints; A3 paper.

What to do

● Read or tell the story of *The Enormous Turnip*. Ask the children to retell the story themselves, sequencing the events. Show them the pieces of the story puzzle from the photocopiable sheet and ask them to put these pieces in a line as they tell the story. When they have finished, ask the children to rearrange the pieces, if they are not already in the correct sequence.

● Invite the children to sit in a circle and take one piece of the puzzle each. Go around the circle, asking them to add to the story by making up one sentence appropriate to their part of the puzzle. For example:

Once upon a time there was a man.

He dug the garden with a fork.

He planted some turnip seeds.

● Support the children by offering suggestions or making up the sentences for

Early writers begin to understand how a story is structured and attempt to write words.
More confident writers sequence a story and write sentences describing one event.

less confident children. As they gain confidence, go around the circle again, telling the story once more.

● Tell the children that you want them to make a big story puzzle for everyone to see. Ask them to take their part of the puzzle and to paint a picture of the character or object on to A3 paper. Once they have completed this, encourage them write the correct naming word under it using paint.

● Display the finished pieces of the puzzle together in a line at child height and let the children enjoy telling the story to each other.

Support and extension

● Encourage younger children to paint over your writing when naming the picture.
● Let older children use thick felt-tipped pens to write a sentence below their pictures.

Further activity

● Ask the children to work with a friend cutting out the pieces of the story puzzle on the photocopiable sheet, mixing them up and gluing them on to a sheet in the correct order.

Home link

Suggest to parents and carers that after reading a story to their child they retell the story together, sequencing the events.

Learning objectives

Stepping Stones
● Use writing as a means of recording and communicating. **(CLL)**
● Begin to be aware of the way stories are structured. **(CLL)**
Early Learning Goals
● Write their own names and other things such as labels and captions and begin to form simple sentences, sometimes using punctuation. **(CLL)**
● Retell narratives in the correct sequence, drawing on language patterns of stories. **(CLL)**

Cross-curricular links

Stepping Stone
Display high levels of involvement in activities. **(PSED)**
Early Learning Goals
● Continue to be interested, excited and motivated to learn. **(PSED)**
● Maintain attention, concentrate and sit quietly when appropriate. **(PSED)**

Story puzzles

man	fork	turnip seeds	watering can
enormous turnip	woman	girl	boy
dog	cat	mouse	enormous turnip

SCHOLASTIC

www.scholastic.co.uk

Story detectives

In this activity, the children begin to understand the shape of a story by acting as detectives working out the storyline from picture clues. They record the story to listen to later.

What you need

'Story detectives' photocopiable page 55 enlarged to A3; tape recorder.

What to do

● Ask the children about occasions when they have gone somewhere for a special day out. Where did they go? What did they take with them?

● Tell the children that you have some clues on a story sheet and you want them to be detectives. Show them the photocopiable sheet and explain that it is a story with a beginning, a middle and an end. But what happens in the story? Tell the group to start at the top and follow the arrows to find out.

● Read the ticket together to discover how many people are in the story and where they are going. Ask the children to think of names for the characters. Which clue tells you what they did first? What was the weather like? What did they buy to help them cool down? What was in the picnic basket? How did they get home?

Early writers use props to help them tell a story.
More confident writers explore key feelings and make a recording of their version of the story.

● When the children have worked out the details of the story, congratulate them on being good detectives and ask them to retell it, using the pictures to help them. Make an audio recording of their version of the story so that they can play it back and listen to it.

Support and extension

● Younger children will find it easier to tell the story using actual objects. Make two tickets and gather together the other items used in the story and tell the story together.

● Older children can describe and add how they think the children in the story were feeling at key moments during the day.

Further activity

● Compose the story together as a group, writing on a large sheet of paper, using different coloured pens for each sentence.

Home link

Encourage parents and carers to help their children collect small items from a walk in the park, and use these to help them tell a simple story.

Learning objectives

Stepping Stones
● Begin to be aware of the way stories are structured. **(CLL)**
● Use talk to connect ideas, explain what is happening and anticipate what might happen next. **(CLL)**

Early Learning Goals
● Retell narratives in the correct sequence, drawing on language patterns of stories. **(CLL)**
● Use talk to organise, sequence and clarify thinking, ideas, feelings and events. **(CLL)**

Cross-curricular links

Stepping Stone
● Display high levels of involvement in activities. **(PSED)**

Early Learning Goals
● Continue to be interested, excited and motivated to learn. **(PSED)**
● Be confident to try new activities, initiate ideas and speak in a familiar group. **(PSED)**

Story detectives

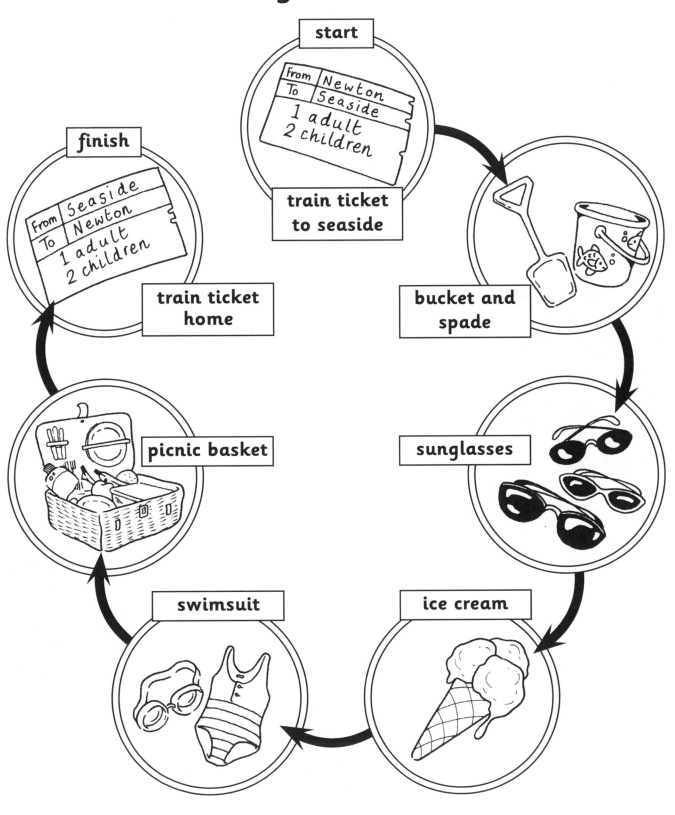

start

From Newton
To Seaside
1 adult
2 children

train ticket to seaside

finish

From Seaside
To Newton
1 adult
2 children

train ticket home

bucket and spade

picnic basket

sunglasses

swimsuit

ice cream

Bananas

In this activity, children use their senses to discover more about bananas and suggest ideas for a simple poem.

What you need
Bunch of five bananas; 'Bunch of bananas' photocopiable page 57 enlarged to A3.

What to do
● Make reading and reciting poetry and rhymes an enjoyable part of each day, so that children become familiar with their variety and structure. Try to include some poems which do not rhyme.

● Children need to have experienced something to inspire them to write a poem. Show the children a bunch of bananas and pass it around the circle for them to observe, touch and smell. (Check with parents and carers first for any food allergies or dietary requirements before carrying out this activity.) Listen to their comments and ask them to describe what the bananas look like, commenting on their colour, shape, weight and size.

● Talk about the words they have used and act as scribe to list some of them. Pass the bananas around the circle twice more, asking the children to comment on what they smell and feel like. Again list the words they use. Finally peel and cut up one banana for them to taste and describe.

● Tell the children that you like their ideas and the words they have used, and you want them to write a poem together about bananas. Poetry has many different forms, but one simple way to introduce writing poetry to young children is to ask them to suggest or write one idea and then start a new line for a new idea.

● Use the banana outline on the photocopiable sheet and discuss with the children what to write on each line. Cross out and change words as the poem develops. Write the finished poem on a new sheet.

Support and extension
● You may find that younger children will need support in describing what they experience.
● Encourage older children to write their own poems using a thick brown felt-tipped pen on the banana template copied on to yellow paper.

Further activity
● Choose a contrasting fruit, such as a pineapple, as a starting point for a poem. Draw the outline of a pineapple and write the poem within it.

Home link
Suggest that parents and carers share poems and rhymes with their children.

> **Early writers** contribute their ideas and begin to understand the concept of a poem.
> **More confident writers** write their own poems within a simple structure.

> **Learning objectives**
> **Stepping Stone**
> ● Use writing as a means of recording and communicating. **(CLL)**
> **Early Learning Goal**
> ● Attempt writing for different purposes, using features of different forms such as lists, stories and instructions. **(CLL)**

> **Cross-curricular links**
> **Stepping Stone**
> ● Examine objects and living things to find out more about them. **(KUW)**
> **Early Learning Goal**
> ● Investigate objects and materials by using all of their senses as appropriate. **(KUW)**

Bunch of bananas

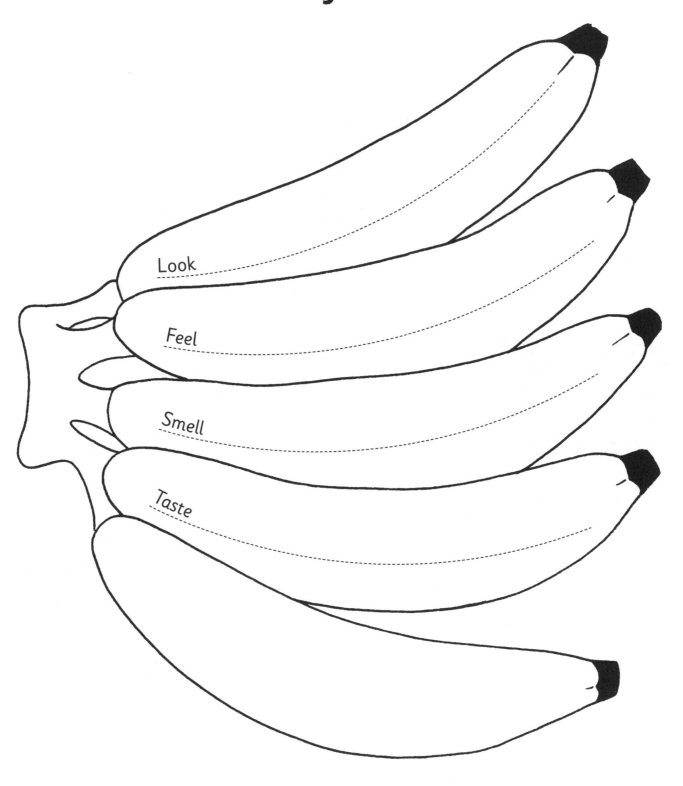

Look ----------------------------------

Feel ----------------------------------

Smell ----------------------------------

Taste ----------------------------------

SCHOLASTIC

www.scholastic.co.uk

At night

Children work together to create a poem about things that can be seen at night. They experiment with words to give different effects and meanings. Their finished poem hangs as a mobile.

What you need

'At night' photocopiable page 59; whiteboard and pens; gold and silver pens; scissors; coat hanger; thread; hole-punch.

What to do

● Talk to the children about the differences between night and day. Ask them to imagine they are outside at night-time and looking up into the sky. What would they see? Which animals come out at night-time and sleep in the day?

● Make a list to include moon, stars, bat, owl and hedgehog. Show the children pictures of these and ask them to think of words to describe them. Write these words on a whiteboard and read them together.

● Explain to the children that you are going to write a night-time poem together. Show them the photocopiable sheet and ask them to give you one idea to write on each cut-out shape to create a poem. Such as:

At night
Stars shine
The moon is bright
Bats fly
Owls hoot
Hedgehogs snuffle

● Spend time talking about and playing

Early writers talk about and paint something associated with night and contribute to a verbal poem.
More confident writers write their own poems.

with the words to create the best effect. Write a line of the poem on the star and moon with a gold pen and on the animals with silver. Make a hole in each shape and hang them at different levels from a coat hanger using fine thread. Attach the title to the top of the coat hanger.

Support and extension

● Invite younger children to draw pictures of things associated with night-time and make a verbal poem together by commenting in turn on their drawings.
● Older children can create their own drawings and poems to hang as mobiles.

Further activity

● Share non-fiction books about nocturnal animals with the children and ask them to draw a picture of one animal using a silver pen on a piece of black A4 paper. They can either write the animal's name below the drawing or write down a fact they have discovered about it.

Home link

Ask parents and carers to accompany their children outside when it is dark so that they can look up at the sky, listen to sounds and perhaps see a bat, owl or hedgehog.

Learning objectives
Stepping Stone
● Respond to simple instructions. **(CLL)**
Early Learning Goal
● Enjoy listening to and using spoken and written language, and readily turn to it in their play and learning. **(CLL)**

Cross-curricular links
Stepping Stone
● Show an interest in what they see, hear, smell, touch and feel. **(CD)**
Early Learning Goal
● Respond in a variety of ways to what they see, hear, smell, touch and feel. **(CD)**

At night

At night

Writing without pencils

SCHOLASTIC
www.scholastic.co.uk

Wash day

Children are introduced to writing a simple alliterative poem about the washing on a line. They pin each line of their poem to items of clothing and read the poem from left to right.

What you need

Toy washing line with a variety of toys' clothes pegged to it; two tea towels; A4 paper; pen; safety pins; digital camera; 'On the washing line' photocopiable page 61.

What to do

● Show the children the washing line and ask them to name one item of clothing and tell you the first sound in that word. Who might it belong to? Listen to their suggestions and then ask them to think of a name beginning with the same sound as the item of clothing, such as 'Sarah's sock'. Encourage them to play around with the sounds and choose one to write on a large label and attach to the end of the sock with a safety pin. Repeat with all the other items.

● Read the labels from left to right and remark that it sounds like a poem. Show the children the photocopiable sheet and read the poem to them. Point out that this poem has a beginning and an end, and suggest that they think of a beginning and end to their poem. Add a tea towel or tablecloth at each end of the washing line and add their ideas. Take a photograph of each part of the finished poem. Print these, hang from a small line indoors and read together.

Support and extension

● Younger children may need support in recognising the initial sounds in words.

● Encourage older children to work with a partner and write their own washing line poems.

Further activity

● Make themed lines of washing and ask the children to work out whose they are. One line could include football shorts, shirts and socks, another could include baby clothes or a line of beachwear after a day at the seaside. Use these as starting points for poems.

Home link

Suggest to parents or carers that they make up nonsense jingles with their children about members of their family, such as: Jack jumps in jelly; Daddy dusts the daffodils and so on.

Early writers are introduced to alliteration as they play with the initial sounds of words and take part in composing a poem together.
More confident writers work with a partner to write their own poems.

Learning objectives
Stepping Stones
● Show awareness of rhyme and alliteration. **(CLL)**
● Know information can be relayed in the form of print. **(CLL)**
Early Learning Goals
● Hear and say initial and final sounds in words, and short vowel sounds within words. **(CLL)**
● Explore and experiment with sounds, words and texts. **(CLL)**

Cross-curricular links
Stepping Stone
● Display high levels of involvement in activities. **(PSED)**
Early Learning Goals
● Continue to be interested, excited and motivated to learn. **(PSED)**
● Be confident to try new activities, initiate ideas and speak in a familiar group. **(PSED)**

On the washing line

On the washing line...

Jim's jeans

Shelly's shirt

Tanya's tights

Simon's socks

Tim's trousers

clean and dry

From my window

Children are encouraged to be observant as they look through a window and to think carefully about the words they use to describe what they see happening outside. They write a simple poem together within the structure of window panes.

What you need
'From my window I can see…'
photocopiable page 63;
felt-tipped pens.

What to do
● Gather the children together around a window. Ask them to tell you what they can see that is moving. Once they have listed various things such as a bird, people, clouds, cars and so on, ask them to tell you what each thing is doing. For example, a bird eating, a man walking, a cloud moving, a car moving.

● Encourage the children to think again about the words they have used and see if they can change any of them to describe more precisely what they are seeing, such as a man hurrying, a bird pecking, a cloud blowing or a car reversing.

● Write the children's ideas in the window panes on the photocopiable sheet. An example is given below:

From my window I can see:

A boy hopping	A cat hiding	A postman walking
A plane flying	A dog barking	A bus stopping
Litter blowing	A baby crying	And rain falling

> **Early writers** talk about and paint what they see, dictating their ideas.
> **More confident writers** work with a partner, writing their own poems.

● Read the poem together. Ask the children if the view from the window will be the same tomorrow. Write a poem on another day or looking through a different window, and compare the two.

Support and extension
● Invite younger children to look through the window and each draw something they see moving. Make a visual poem by sticking their pictures inside each window pane on the photocopiable sheet and adding their captions.
● Older children can work with a partner to write their own poems using felt-tipped pens.

Further activity
● Watch other children playing and write a poem together about what they are doing, for example:
I can see…
Joshua climbing
Makayla painting
Alfie skipping
Robert laughing
Lili singing
and Isabelle dancing.

Home link
Suggest that parents and carers encourage their children to be observant, and talk about things they see in everyday situations such as shopping or going to the park.

Learning objectives
Stepping Stones
● Begin to recognise some familiar words. **(CLL)**
● Begin to break the flow of speech into words. **(CLL)**
Early Learning Goals
● Explore and experiment with sounds, words and texts. **(CLL)**
● Attempt writing for different purposes, using features of different forms such as lists, stories and instructions. **(CLL)**

Cross-curricular links
Stepping Stone
● Show an interest in the world in which they live. **(KUW)**
Early Learning Goal
● Observe, find out about and identify features in the place they live and the natural world. **(KUW)**

From my window I can see...

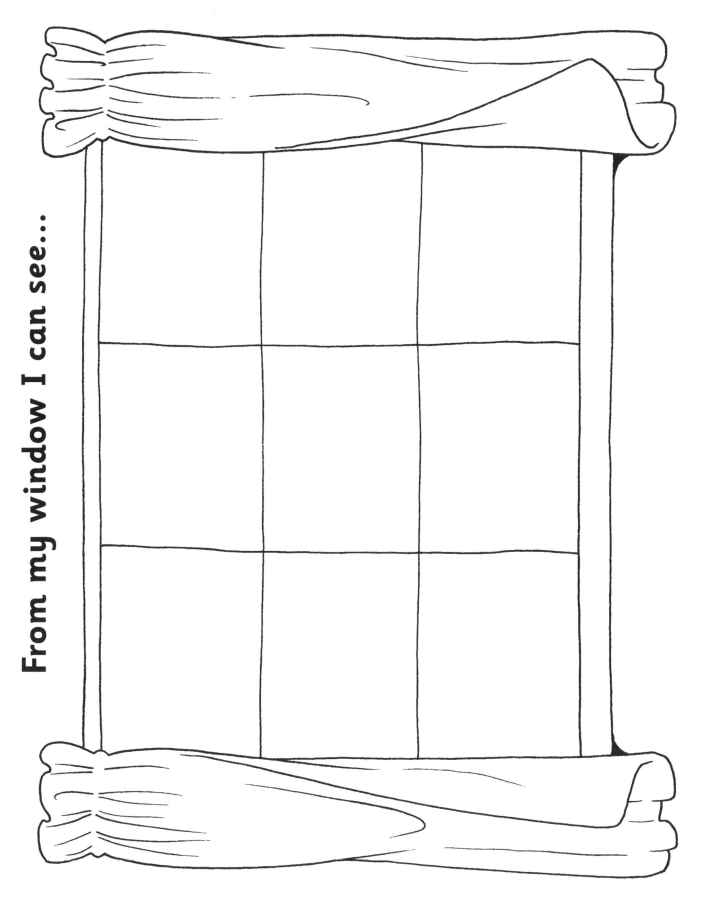

SCHOLASTIC
www.scholastic.co.uk